Social Media

The Ultimate Marketing Strategies for Beginners

Table of Contents

Introduction

I want to thank you and congratulate you for purchasing this book...

"Social Media: The Ultimate Marketing Strategies for Beginners"

This book will help you get acquainted with social media marketing for business. By discussing what social media is, how it can be used other than for personal networking, and what different platforms are available for you to utilize, I hope that you will gain valuable knowledge on how to take advantage of this innovation to promote your brand and boost your business over time.

Thanks again for purchasing this book, I hope you enjoy it!

Chapter 1. Social Media in a Nutshell

Websites like Facebook, Twitter, and Instagram to name a few allow companies to build relationships and communities with targeted audiences over the Web. Consumers now have the ability to interact more closely with potential clients regardless of their distance. It allows for a more personal level of interaction between brands and their followers.

When companies engage via social media, they attract word-of-mouth advertising when followers talk about or share their content on their personal pages. With the Internet offering an unlimited and international audience reach, this is one of the most powerful tools that any company can utilize. As more people share content and comment on whatever you publish, the brand gets more attention thereby increasing potential conversions.

Social Media and Demographic Targeting

Social media websites work by helping you build communities on a virtual level where people can express their needs and wants with ease. Through social media marketing, these people get connected with different companies that offer solutions to these needs and wants.

Social media platforms also make it easier for these businesses to start and maintain relevant communication with their prospects. It also allows for personal interactions which a lot of consumers prefer. Especially when companies work with multiple product offerings, each with a different target market, they can launch campaigns online targeting specific demographics saving time, effort, and money.

With the help of semantic analytics, you can easily figure out what types of things your prospects might be interested in. Through their shared content, you can catch a glimpse of the products they are into or the services that they are willing to pay for. This now gives you an idea on how to better approach these people, based on the buying signals that you get, potentially earning you more conversions online.

Social Media on the Go

Aside from accessing social media sites on laptops, a majority of people access these through their mobile phones. Mobile phones are very important when it comes to social media marketing because these offer 24/7 reach. Doing so, you are then able to reach prospects and update them as soon as you deem necessary. There are no wait times to release a new promo or introduce a new product.

Consumers, on the other hand, can quickly learn about whatever it is you are offering by conducting a Web search on the same phones giving them the information that they need to immediately react to your post. A great tool for you to use here would be QR (quick response) codes. These are the matrix barcodes that automatically lead people to specific landing pages through a simple picture taken on mobile phones connected to the Web.

Embracing the Concept of Social Media

Did you know that given these modern times, deciding not to rely on social media for active promotion can be detrimental to your business? There are plenty of advantages that come with using social media to market products and services of all sorts.

You might find it somewhat tough to stomach but there are plenty of businesses that have started to embrace the concept of social media marketing for a ton of reasons, one of them being brand building. This is why you should find the time to check various social media channels out for your own company.

Plenty of the companies that have since included social media channels in their marketing efforts have clung to traditional modes of advertising for so long that some of their chosen promotional styles can already be deemed as obsolete.

Not having the right social media networks working on your behalf can already be compared with not having a cellphone in this modern day and age. You will pass up and miss out on plenty of opportunities for B2B (business to business) and B2C (business to consumer) linking.

As the days go by, you will experience more harm than security for your business. You don't have to be fully on board with all social media networks but must be open to at least utilizing one or two avenues regularly.

The Advantages of Social Media

Without social media, there will be a lot of people who won't get to know how amazing your brand is. Even if you have a small loyal customer base, you have to understand that this will not be enough if you wish for your business to go places.

1. The more people who know your business, the better.

    Businesses can routinely share updates, customer testimonials, and other valuable content via social media and fast. In turn, happy customers add to the promotion by sharing positive experiences linked to your business on their personal social media pages.

2. Social media also enables you to know what people are saying about you.

You will have both happy and unhappy clients and these people will constantly leave feedback online. If you are not present in any social media channel, you won't get any vital information when you need it the most. This will limit you from addressing the problem or doing any crowd control.

You will also miss out on the opportunity to engage with satisfied clients which in turn is not a good thing. With engagement being an essential business component these days, you have to stay connected and be responsive to your customers and potential clients.

3. You can improve your engagement with clients through social media channels because they connect you to these people on a more direct and personal level.

What's even better is that they can reach you with ease and you can respond within minutes. The more you engage with your clientele, the more traction your business will gain over time. You can also gain valuable information that can help you improve your offerings even more by speaking with these consumers.

4. It helps you cut your costs on advertising.

Traditional media outlets cost tons to penetrate while social media is often free lest you decide to use pay per click or impression ads. Even so, the costs are generally lower even if it does get you wider audience reach.

Also, ads are easy to program and launch. A couple of hours and you are well on your way to launching an ad which you can also monitor and tweak as often as you wish.

5. Aside from introducing your brand via ads or organic content, social media can also help you build and establish a credible reputation as a thought leader online.

If you are an expert in your industry yet not enough people hear about you then your efforts will not be as powerful as they can be. If you happen to have news, updates, new product information, you won't effectively be able to spread the word without social media as well. If you are able to do so, it will only be a limited audience not all of which are potential customers.

6. You are more likely to have information on what your competitors are doing if you are present in the online sphere.

   Don't assume that just because you are not online that competitors are offline as well. If you are able to monitor their social media networks then you will have an idea as to what they are up to, what campaigns they are planning on running, and how they engage with your target audience. This information could be essential especially when you are developing your marketing strategies.

7. Being active on social media can also help you find quality employees.

   You can reach more talented professionals by advertising vacancies on your social media sites especially on Facebook. If you have a vibrant online presence, you are also making yourself more attractive to potential employees as this gives them the impression that you are going with the tide, open to new and modern things, and so on.

8. Finally, you don't want to get caught in any type of crisis without social media backing you up.

   Crises are part of business as you cannot make every customer happy. In one way or another you will experience hurdles in your operations may it be through product-related problems or public relations issues. When this time comes, you want to have an active social media following that can help you gain more control of the situation.

You don't want to be tagged as a company that ignores complaints so by being able to address problems in a timely manner while reaching the largest crowd possible, you can help yourself bounce back by integrating crisis management with your social media strategy. You can easily dispel rumors, speculation, and the like in one tweet and call it a day.

You can address product concerns through a simple Facebook post and clear things up. You can quiet down angry voices by being available for comment and by responding to those who have a question or two.

Chapter 2. The Basic Rules of Social Media Marketing

Regardless of the type of business that you run, there is always a way for you to leverage the power of social media. Doing so, you are opening more doors to increase your customer base. Beginners might find the task quite challenging but it is an obstacle worth undertaking.

The important thing is that you understand that the use of social media, just like other marketing tools, has its set of fundamentals which you must familiarize yourself with. Start with these ten basic rules and take them to heart. They will help you establish a strong foundation that will aid you in serving your clients and building your brand in the ever-competitive online space.

1. Listen to your audience

When it comes to social media platforms, one of the most important things to do is listen. Even if you are there to deliver sound content to your prospects, you have to do more listening than talking. This is how you can fully comprehend your market, what their desires are, what they are interested in, and what gets them talking.

This is how you can develop a strategy that will work by generating high levels of engagement online. Remember that the ultimate goal is not to add clutter to their lives but provide something of value that they would want to share with other potential customers.

2. Focus

With plenty of heavy competition across markets these days, it is always better to specialize in your chosen field. The same goes for your social media strategy where you should prioritize a highly-focused and targeted campaign at all times. Doing so will lead you to more success for your efforts.

3. Never Compromise Quality

Whenever you create any type of content via text, image, or video, you should remember that quality is extremely important. Concentrate your efforts on creating something valuable that even first-time connections would consider sharing with others. The goal is to gain and maintain connections. You do not want people disappearing from your circle after the initial lockdown.

4. Be Patient

Like any kind of marketing campaign, it will take time for a social media tactic to achieve results. This is why you should be patient. Nothing happens overnight and you should not expect your situation to be different. Keep your expectations at a reasonable level especially if this is your first time utilizing social media platforms for business purposes.

5. Compound Your Reach

When it comes to social media marketing, campaigns are not independent of one another. They work side by side to build an audience, a loyal following, over time. This means that you should create content that will help compound your online reach. This means providing valuable resources that will be shared and reposted by other people on their own social media accounts and communities. Create something that goes viral and you'll be all set!

Aside from growing your social media presence, taking advantage of this type of compounding will also help you boost your search engine rankings as your identity becomes more noticeable via keyword searches.

6. Get Influencers on Your Team

Influencers are people, not necessarily celebrities that have large followings sometimes even on a global scale. It will be a good idea for you to connect with these individuals as it will help you build your brand through their endorsement.

7. Always Add Value

Even if you are online for business, constantly promoting your products will not get you the attention and following that you can benefit from. On the other hand, hard-selling can only lead you to lose people over time. Always add value to every conversation. Focus on delivering valuable content and you will get desirable conversions. Continue doing this and you will get an unbelievable amount of word-of-mouth advertising for your brand.

8. Acknowledge Your Audience

By going online, surely your goal is to be recognized. When people do start recognizing your brand, do not fail to acknowledge them. Especially when people start to engage, be sure to reach out, reply, and service their queries in a timely manner.

9. Be Accessible to Your Prospects

Regularly update your social media accounts with valuable content but do not stop there. When these attract attention and engagement, always be available to those who respond. Be available to your audience so when you publish something, participate in the conversations that follow. Disappear even for a few days and you will lose valuable followers.

10. Reciprocate

Social media is pretty much like dancing the tango. You create content and expect people to share it on your behalf so you have to reciprocate by sharing content from other sources every now and then. Set aside a portion of your time to share and talk about other's content.

Chapter 3. Social Media Marketing Approaches

There are two primary approaches that you can use when marketing via social media. There are the passive and active strategies that you can put into play. The passive approach is gentler yet yields vital information like market movements, consumer behavior, and preference data.

Through blogs, forums, and content sharing, companies are able to listen to their prospects' views on products and services and derive ample strategies from there. Businesses are given countless opportunities to tap into the minds of their consumers and hear what they have to say in a discrete fashion.

And then there is the active approach which involves using social media as a means to improve direct communication between brands and consumers. Aside from targeting social media influencers, this strategy might include companies focusing on direct target audiences as well. This kind of approach involves the use of live ads, paid or free, which are hyper-targeted to a specific demographic.

When you decide on using social media for your business, you also have to consider finding the best platform to focus your attention on. Although there are multiple channels available, this does not mean that you should use all of them. In some cases, there are channels which might not be as effective for your brand as it is for others. So why waste your time and energy on these?

If this is your first time using social media platforms for marketing purposes, spend time testing these out. Also look into what your competitors are doing. This will help you narrow down your options and will also provide you with valuable insight as to which types of content or campaigns can generate the noise that you require.

Start by asking yourself three simple questions. What behavior are you trying to drive and what business goal do you wish to achieve? Which of the available social media platforms can best highlight my products or services? Who are my target consumers and how do they behave on the Internet?

When you have resolved these queries, shift your attention to what your community needs and worry less about what is popular as these may not always be relevant in your industry or general market.

Chapter 4. Engagement

The thing about social media is that it makes direct engagement a possibility between brands and consumers. In this case, both are participants in active and timely conversations. Businesses are able to reach their markets with ease and these consumers are able to express their thoughts or opinions on the products and services being offered. You can say that consumers become members of the company's research and marketing team in more ways than one.

There are two components to social media engagement starting with the proactive posting of relevant and valuable content. This includes posting and sharing not only self-published content but conversations and information from other sources as well. And then there is the reactive strategy which focuses mainly on striking conversations and engaging in discussions with brand followers online.

What makes engagement all the more effective via social media is the fact that it is not like traditional media that is limited to one-way interactions between companies and their clients. The latter only allows for their desired information to be disseminated without opening doors to welcome usable feedback.

Social media marketing on the other hand values and encourages participation shifting most of the message control to the consumers instead of exclusively holding it for companies.

Chapter 5. Twitter

A couple of years after Facebook was launched, a new platform by the name of Twitter came to light. Twitter was founded in 2006 and has since transformed how people gained access to information in real time.

Twitter works by allowing companies to promote their offerings with the use of short messages known globally as tweets. A tweet is limited to 140 characters (spaces included) and when published appear on the timelines of their followers.

Aside from text, a tweet can also contain images, videos, animated GIFs, emoji's, or product site links. It can also be connected with other social media profiles if necessary.

Hashtags can be used to highlight specific keywords that can be used for searches on the platform giving non-followers the ability to access company tweets for as long as the latter's account is set to public mode. Hashtags are written by creating a word or phrase starting with the # symbol. These hashtags are indexed, making it possible for users to follow the topics they're interested in.

Source: appsglossy.com

What makes this social media outlet different from the rest is that it only comes with bite-sized updates that measure in at 140 characters but can deliver tons of information from current news to personal messages.

There is plenty of information that can be obtained from the Internet but with the help of direct updates and hashtags, people can easily find what they need via Twitter.

This being said, a number of brands and companies these days have started using this platform not only for promotional messages but also for immediate updates that address the needs of their clientele.

Platform Statistics

It is popular amongst an equal percentage of men and women with 72% of its active users falling between the ages of 18 and 49. With a recorded 400 million tweets sent out per day, this just shows you how relevant of a social media platform Twitter is making it an excellent tool for corporate marketing.

To develop an effective social media marketing strategy using Twitter, you must first familiarize yourself with how people, including your potential audience, are using the platform.

You should know that is has and continues to replace everything from RSS subscriptions to traditional news media. It's highly public nature is responsible for the service efficiently and effectively connecting people from around the world allowing strangers to come together over common ideas and interests. It makes participating in conversations fast, easy, and convenient.

Creating and Using Your Twitter Account

- Here are the steps to creating your account:

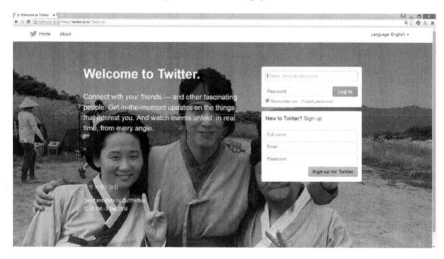

1. Go to https://twitter.com and sign up by entering your full name, email address, and a chosen password.

2. After clicking the sign up button, you will be transferred to a verification page. Input your mobile number to receive the SMS.

16

3. A code will be sent to your mobile number. Enter it on the box provided.

4. Once your account has been verified, you can then select a username. The site will tell you if your chosen handle is already in use.

5. Double-check your name, phone number, password, and username.

6. Finish the process by clicking the "Create My Account" button. Depending on your system, you might be asked to complete a Captcha.

7. Complete the registration process by verifying the account via a confirmation message that will be sent to your email address.

Tips for picking a Twitter handle:

1. Your username is the name that will be used by your followers when sending you @replies and direct messages. It will also serve as part of your Twitter page's URL so choose the perfect name that resonates with your business.

2. You can change your username anytime for as long as the new handle is still available.

3. Usernames need to be less than 15 characters and cannot contain the words "admin" or "Twitter."

Twitter Basics and Sending Out That First Tweet:

1. Once your account has been created, log in using your chosen credentials then complete your profile by uploading a cover photo and profile image to further establish your brand identity.

2. On the middle of the interface is a "What's happening" tab. Click on it to enter a message or upload images, links, and the like. Click on the "Tweet" button at the lower right hand side of the tab to send out your first tweet. The same button can also be found on the top right hand corner of the main interface. You can also click on that to open a tweet window.

3. On the left hand side of the interface are your stats from your tweets, following, and followers. Above that are the home, notifications, and messages buttons. A red dot will appear on top of them when there are contents or updates that you haven't seen yet.

4. You will find the latest trending hashtags on the left hand side of the interface as well. These topics are what Twitter users are actively talking about within a 24 hour window.

5. On the right hand side of the interface are users that you might be interested in following based on the interests that you ticked off during the registration process.

6. Below the list of who to follow is the "advertise with us" button should you choose to advertise with Twitter. Click on it and you will be led to a step-by-step ad creation window.

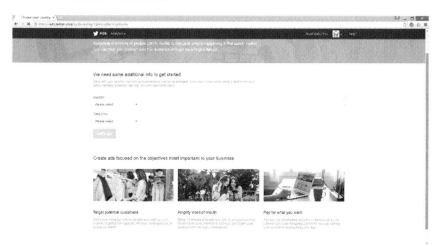

7. Click on your profile image on the top right hand corner of the interface and you will have access to everything from your profile to your account's analytics, ads, and settings tabs.

The Initial Approach

Here are some of the things that you should consider when establishing your business' presence on twitter:

1. Start your research by participating in various chats that are on topics that revolve around the interests of your target market and brand. This will help you expand your network. Be observant of the hashtags being used in these conversations.

2. Take advantage of tools such as the platform's built-in Discovery function to find relevant conversations. They also offer a Categories function which allows you to browse different accounts based on the topics you choose.

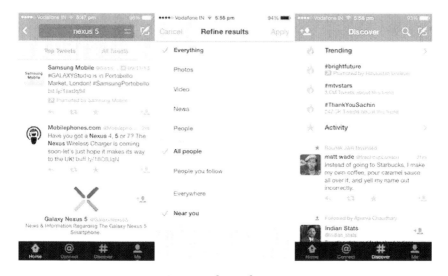

Source: gadgets.ndtv.com

3. You will find users that regularly update their accounts. There are other people though that limit their activity to sharing content or "retweeting" as it is formally called. The ultimate goal is for you to identify which of these users you should be engaging with.

    You should understand how they are using the platform so that you can develop the best engaging strategy for your campaign. Like other brands, surely you have a primary objective, and your success on Twitter will depend on this and your manner of approaching it.

4. Remember that you are limited to 140 characters per tweet. You should see to it that your brand's voice is communicated given this allotted number of characters. You don't have to blatantly mention your name or tagline as there are users who don't like hard-sellers.

    What you can do is pattern your tweets in such a way that you are able to sway them towards the direction of whatever it is you are promoting. One of the best strategies to consider is appealing to their emotions. Once you are able to tug at their heartstrings, all you have to do is reel them in.

21

Twitter is a highly active social network so you want to be visible all day and all week. Schedule meaningful messages, shared or original, at least three times a day to start; one in the morning, at noon, and in the afternoon.

5. When working on any type of engagement, you should never compromise consistency. Your audience should know what to expect from you in terms of content. They should also have an idea of how to interact with you. By remaining consistent, you will be able to establish a sense of trust over time not to mention improve your market's level of confidence when it comes to your brand.

6. Consistency does not only apply to your content schedule. Being consistent also means making sure that your profile is up to date and of course, correct. Be careful of what you put in your bio as it should reflect your brand in the most truthful way possible.

   Even the location that you indicate should be as accurate as possible. Control your follower-following ratio as well. As a business, you should have more followers than followed profiles. Also be careful of who you are following.

7. Be as responsive as possible too. Twitter runs at a quick pace and this is why you should response to comments or tweets within a short period of time especially when you are dealing with customer service concerns. Do say hello or give thanks as well especially when your content is shared by other users.

8. Analytics are important here. Do measure the responsiveness of your tweets. By tracking engagement, you will know which types of content or approaches work enabling you to create a better social media marketing strategy over time. Test out content twice a month to start.

Twitter Best Practices

There are best practices that can be applied to all sorts of social media platforms. When it comes to Twitter, here are some of the general guidelines that you should always have at the back of your mind.

1. Avoid delivering spammy content. This applies to all of your marketing efforts. Spam content pertains to repetitive content. No matter how legitimate the brand is, if the marketer resorts to spam content, this will drive away followers faster than a flick of a switch.

   Spam content also pertains to the use of irrelevant hashtags when it comes to this platform. For example, if you are talking about a bicycle, you should not use a hashtag linked to a dog.

   You might think that linking your content with trending hashtags will help your efforts but in reality, it will do you more harm than good. Another type of spamming involves mentioning your peers or followers, by name, in several consecutive posts.

2. Twitter has a direct messaging feature but you can only send DMs to the people that you follow and are following you. Use this when dealing with sensitive information like personal contact details or requests for addresses and the like. Do your best to keep each DM personal. Steer clear of automated ones. Not only will this be seen as non-engaging but can also be considered as spam.

   Whenever you utilize the DM feature, always remember to be engaging and to keep conversations as personal as possible but don't forget relevance and the provision of value.

   If you are sending out a specific reply and use an @ symbol, unless you place a period (.) or other type of marker after the username, only your followers that

23

follow the private individual will be able to see the tweet.

3. And then there are hashtags (#) which have already been mentioned. The rule is pretty simple with this one. Use relevant hashtags depending on the content you will be posting. There are plenty of online sources that you can check for the latest and trending hashtags available. This will give you a gauge as to what people are talking about or looking for.

Scheduling Content on Twitter

Twitter is one of those social media platforms that allow for scheduled content although you need a third-party scheduler. Scheduling content is a great advantage especially if you are working on a brand that requires consistent account updating. This allows you to schedule everything at one go then start work on other things on your list.

If you plan on doing this, be sure that you are still updated as to what content will be published and what current news are taking place. If you have a scheduled post that might be offensive given a current tragedy or mishap, shut it off immediately. You wouldn't want a single tweet to create an inhospitable environment. You don't want to make yourself the center of controversy.

Other Tools on Twitter

The platform allows for list generation so use it. By making a list of users, you can improve your targeting efforts on Twitter especially if you are trying to reach a certain demographic of consumers. Use lists to be inclusive and not the other way around. Do not use public lists for the purpose of rating people or other brands. If you require such a function, it is best to create a private list that won't cause negative small talk.

Twitter cards are also available. You use this by setting up your online content with specific Meta data. Doing so, you will turn ordinary content to rich content whenever someone uses its link in a tweet. There are different types of cards readily available on the platform. Try them out to see which one works best for your brand. Some cards even go the extra mile by helping businesses drive conversions to their pages by having a clear call to action.

Chapter 6. Facebook

Facebook profiles allow for more details. The platform also allows for longer descriptions or text to be displayed per post. Aside from GIFs, videos, hashtags, and links, it is also possible to create and post photo albums on the platform.

Each post is provided with three buttons for liking, commenting, and sharing. Consumers can like a post, leave their feedback underneath the content, or share the entire post to their personal pages with the click of a button. It is an excellent and fast way of having your content shared in cyberspace.

Facebook also offers advertising solutions for businesses. You can boost responsive posts or create sponsored ads depending on the campaign or business strategy that you are currently working with.

Simply plot out the details, add images or videos, set your budget, and choose your demographic and you are ready to have your ads published on the platform.

Source: www.baltzersens.co.uk

Facebook started back in 2004. It was created by a student by the name of Mark Zuckerberg. It started out as a bare-boned social networking platform that served to connect college students but quickly gained traction over the masses.

In less than a decade after it was initially launched, the platform was able to gain over than a billion users from around the globe making it the most widely-used social networking platform that has yet to be overtaken by any predecessor or up and coming network.

Platform Statistics

There was a reported 1.19 billion active monthly users on the platform as of June 2013. 59% of these users that "like" brand pages are reportedly comprised of individuals who have already purchased a product or experienced a service being offered by a business. 45% of users "like" these same pages when doing so means getting promotional benefits or rewards.

These stats are vital information to any company. This gives you an idea of how to mold your campaign to attract the attention that you need on the Web. Basically, these are the details that you should focus on when you draft that initial Facebook strategy.

With an average of 4.5 billion "likes" being generated on a daily basis, there is no reason for you not to give this free-to-use platform a try for your own online marketing needs.

Creating and Using Your Facebook Account

Here are the steps to create your Facebook account:

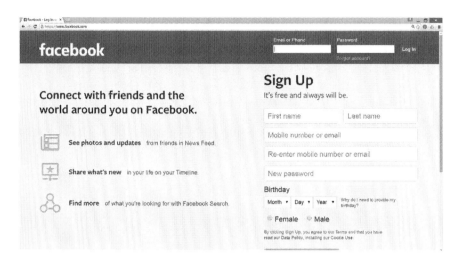

1. Go to https://www.facebook.com and click on "Sign Up."

2. Fill out the sign up form by inputting your name, email address, phone number, password, birthday, and gender.

3. When you send the filled out form, you will receive a confirmation email or SMS. Click on the link provided to confirm your account.

When creating Facebook pages for multiple products or brands, you will undergo a similar process:

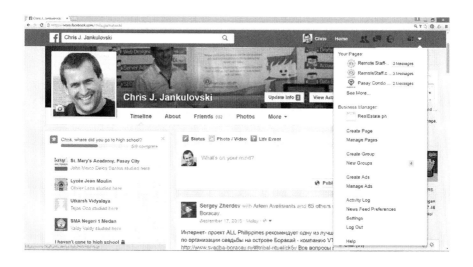

1. Click on the bottom facing arrow on the top right hand corner of the interface then select "Create Page."

2. You will then be transferred to a step-by-step interface to create your new page which can then be accessed under your primary account via "Manage Pages."

** You may use the same process to create Facebook groups.

How to create advertisements on Facebook

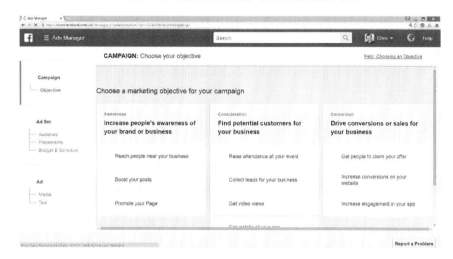

1. Click on the bottom facing arrow on the top right hand corner of the interface then select "Create Ads."

2. You will then be transferred to a step-by-step interface to create your ads which can then be monitored under your primary account via "Manage Ads."

Interface and Basic Facebook Access Points

Every time you log into your Facebook account, you will encounter an interface with multiple buttons.

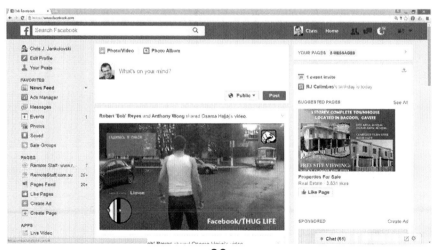

1. You can instantly post content by filling out the "What's on your mind?" tab in the center. You can upload text, links, images, and other media formats here. You can also set the privacy limiting who sees what you will be posting. Click on post and have your content published immediately.

2. There's a search tab on the top left hand side of the interface where you can look for people, content, and trending topics.

3. The left hand section also carries quick links to the different feature elements of Facebook.

4. The middle section is where you will find your general home feed consisting of posts from the people in your friends list.

5. On the right side you will find your events and other notifications. It also carries suggested pages and sponsored ads.

6. Click on the chat window on the bottom to open the chat window where you can instantly converse with active friends.

7. Click on the earth icon on the top right hand corner to see your notifications. This includes updates on friends' posts, activity on your posts, and other important notifications.

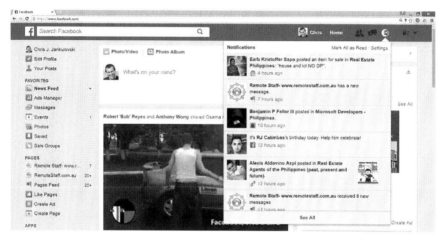

8. The two other icons beside the earth icon are for friend requests (people silhouette) and messages (message bubble).

9. Beside the earth icon is a padlock where you can access your account's security and privacy settings.

10. The bottom facing arrow will lead you to the main access menu where you can find links to your pages, groups, ads, settings, analytics, and the like.

11. Click on your name and you will be directed to your page where you can see all of your posts and account information via the tabs on the center of the interface.

When to Use Facebook

What you should know about Facebook though is that it offers more than just an avenue for posting content and sharing posts. Here are some of the things that people, private individuals and businesses, regularly use Facebook for.

1. If you are planning on setting up a business page on Facebook, take advantage of its "groups" feature. These are user-created communities that vary depending on security and privacy. These groups can be organized around various topics from professional inclination to special interests or niches.

2. Aside from creating groups for your products (if you have various products or brands under your umbrella), you can also join groups that match the industry that you belong to or the products and services that you are offering.

33

Source: www.news.com.au

3. You can also use it to promote company events. Facebook has an "events" calendar that you can use. Simply name the event, input the date, time, and location, provide more details, and then publish it on your wall. You can choose to set the audience to public or private depending on what the event is.

The great thing about it is that the people you send it out to can click buttons on whether they are coming, not coming, or still deciding on going or not. This will give you an idea on how many people to expect.

facebook
Search
The Royal Wedding
Share · Public event
Time
29 April · 11:00 - 14:00
Location
Westminster Abbey
Created by:
The British Monarchy
More info
Will you be taking part in the Royal Wedding celebrations? Whether you're coming to central London to line the route with millions of others or at home in front of the TV with a few select friends, click 'I'm attending' to show your interest in the event and to receive the latest updates and info about Prince William and Catherine Middleton's big day.

Source: www.natashajudd.com

4. If you are handling multiple brands under one company, you can create several business pages to have one designated profile for each of these brands. Unlike personal pages, these are equipped with more tools and functionalities that make is easier for marketers to meet their goals using the platform. It carries elements such as analytics, security, access, reporting, and advertising.

Content Scheduling and Facebook Best Practices

As more companies join the bandwagon and utilize Facebook for their social media marketing efforts, an increase in noise levels for individual users can be expected as a result.

Take note that news feeds for individuals are customized based on their interests and what is popular. With a ton of content being filtered out by the platform day in and day out, you really need to focus on creating posts that will stand out lest be lost in the wind.

Here are some strategies that you might want to look into to work your way up the ladder of Facebook success.

1. As what was previously discussed, it is vital that you provide valuable content at all times. Concentrate on what your target's interests are but never forget to deliver content that is relevant to your brand. You cannot successfully market a travel product by posting content about car parts even if it is about a Lambo or what not.

2. Most Facebook users are visually motivated. This means that photos, videos, and GIFs will garner you the most traction per post compared to plain text posts. The catchier the media, the better the reaction and responsiveness will be. On average, these types of posts get 39% more engagement so keep this figure in mind.

3. Timing is also important when it comes to Facebook posts. Back in the day, you had to post content manually but then third-party scheduling sites started popping up. These days, Facebook has its own post scheduler which you can use to schedule posts on your page. Imagine the ease of scheduling posts for an entire month in just a couple of hours!

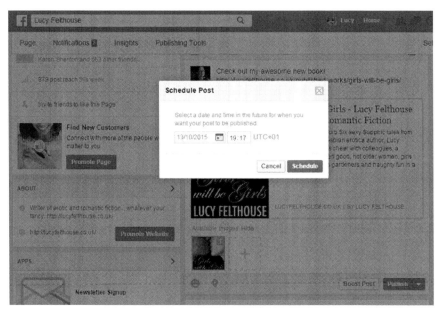

4. Using the analytics feature in your page, check which times of day your followers are most responsive. Yes, times, because it is always best to post more than once daily especially if you are promoting a new brand, product, or service. Doing so ensures that you reach as many people as possible without having to pay for sponsored ads that are blasted throughout the day.

   Facebook users behave differently but it will be good to start with a morning post, around 8AM, one during lunch at around 12 noon, and one in the afternoon at about 5PM when people get off from work. Start by posting content from Mondays through to Fridays as there is less traction during the weekends. If you are intent on being visible on weekends as well, one post a day scheduled in the morning will be good to test out.

5. Posting content, no matter how good it is, will not be as effective if you don't regularly manage your pages. You have to check for comments and feedback. Are people "liking" you page? Which types of content are regularly shared? Are there comments for you to respond to?

6. Remember that Facebook, like most social media platforms, is considered to be an open and highly public space. This means that you cannot control what people say about your brand may it be negative in nature. Do not simply delete these comments or ban these people from your page (unless necessary). Come up with respectful and informative responses that offer solutions to their issues and queries.

   Do not allow messages to stand unread for a long time. A response time of 2 hours is acceptable but it would be better if you can shorten this as you move forward. There are different management apps that you can download on your mobile device to help you easily access these comments and quickly respond to them on-the-go.

7. When you start building your brand online, do not forget that your credibility is also being put under the limelight. A huge part of any brand is founded on trust so be careful when it comes to your spelling and grammar as a simple typo or misuse of words can be interpreted negatively by some followers. When sharing facts and news, check all sources for legitimacy. Be wary of malicious content as well.

8. Do share a wide array of content focusing on the interests of your consumers but do so in such a way that it steers them towards the direction that you want them to take which is supporting your brand by buying your products or availing of your services loyally.

We've been discussing value and all and this is really the most important component of social media marketing but you should use it in such a way that still helps your brand generate the kind of awareness that it needs to thrive.

Chapter 7. Google Plus

Google is probably the most popular search engine on the Internet. Google+ is integrated into the Google search engine and offers its users the ability to create pages and take advantage of tools that have also been popularized by Facebook.

It is a Google product that allows for targeted advertising most of which focus on location-based marketing and promotion. The best part is that it helps companies improve their search engine rankings via SEO or search engine optimization.

Google Plus is a social media platform that is highly relevant, effective, and efficient but is often taken for granted. If you have decided to leave it be, think again as you might be making a huge and costly mistake.

Source: www.northnationmedia.com

Relatively new, Google Plus only hit the scene in 2011. Google was smart. Instead of worrying about developing a platform from scratch, they adopted various features from their predecessors mainly Twitter and Facebook.

It came with distinct features though namely Hangouts and Circles. Unlike other social media networks, this one acts as Google's main social component working closely with the search engine's other elements like its active ad network.

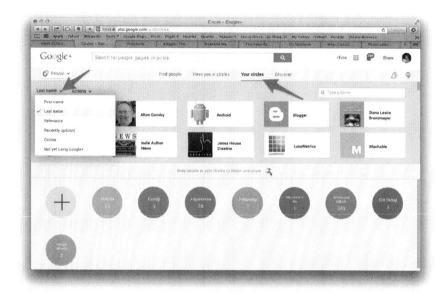

Source: thewriteconversation.blogspot.com

Platform Statistics

Clouded by the appealing features not to mention the popularity of its predecessors, people lose track of the fact that Google continues to exist as the primary search engine used on a global scale. Google Plus content passes link equity to other pages and this is what helps improve a brand's pages' rankings online. These are reasons you should build a strong presence here.

When you take a closer look at the numbers, there are over 300 million active users here with about 2 million photos alone published weekly add to this other shared content. Its predecessors have a relatively equal mix of males and females when it comes to users but this one has been recorded to have a following measuring in at 70% male and 30% female. If your brand revolves around education, student life, photography, and technology then this platform is worth investing in.

Creating and Using Your Google Plus Account

Here are the steps to create your Google Plus account:

1. Go to http://plus.google.com and click on 'Create an Account." It is the red button on the top corner of the interface and is pretty hard to miss.

2. Fill in all of the required information then click on "Next Step."

3. Add your profile photo and a cover photo for your page. Click on "Next Step" and you will have a Google Plus account.

- You can create pages under your main account:

1. Simply go to http://plus.google.com/pages/create and you will be directed to a page creation wizard.

2. Identify the type of page that you want to create then go through the profile set up process similar to the one you encountered when you created your primary account.

3. All of your pages can be accessed through your main account.

Accessing and navigating your stream:

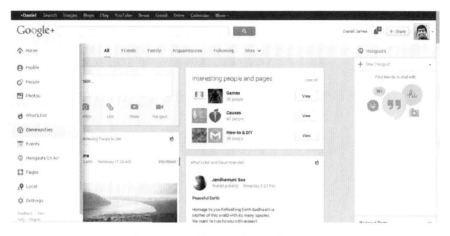

Source: http://www.authormedia.com/

1. Log in to your Google Plus account.

2. You will then see your account's page with all the incoming posts from the people you follow.

3. Using the gray bar on the top, easily switch between feeds from your circles.

4. On the top right hand corner will be your profile.

5. The bell is your notifications icon. A red numbered square will appear every time you have unread updates.

6. Click on the bell to expand the notifications tab and check your updates.

7. Click on your profile image to get the links to your account and privacy settings.

8. Use the tabs above the feeds to access your Google Plus data from your posts to photos, videos, and reviews.

Posting content

Source: http://www.authormedia.com/

1. Click the "Home" button on the top left hand side of the interface.

2. Click on the "Share What's New" box and type in whatever content you wish.

3. You can include images, videos, events, or links to the post if necessary.

4. There is no character limit here and line spacing can be used as well.

5. You can set the post to public or shared to specific people. For the latter, add their Google Plus handles on the "To" box.

6. You can also send an update about the post to your friends by ticking the check box below.

7. Select "Share" and publish your content.

Google Special Features

Engagement on this platform works in about the same way as Twitter or Facebook but because of the availability of the Circles functionality, page owners have the ability to force-categorize people making the platform highly customizable and flexible yet private. This element makes it easy for marketers to reach wider audiences with ease.

There is also the Hangouts feature. You can set this to public or invite-only mode. Through this component, you can establish communities enabling people to interact with one another without having to download any type of software or follow one or the other on Google Plus.

Sources: www.ubergizmo.com

The Initial Approach

In this social network, success does not mainly depend on your content. It also depends on your network, your audience. If you plan on utilizing this platform, see to it that you have done your research. You will not be successful if your target market is not making use of it.

1. It is always a good idea to brainstorm. In this case, what you should do is gather influencers not only relevant to the brand but any specific product as well and create a community for these people to converse in. Use this forum to get the necessary feedback or insights that you need for whatever it is you are offering. Communities you created are tagged back to your main profile so this gives you an additional layer of marketing via engagement.

2. Aside from this, get that traction you need via interactive events posts. Here is where you can invite users to events. Should they choose to RSVP, the event will be tagged on their calendar. The events function enables you to improve your online presence while developing your offline visibility as well.

3. As you create your Google Plus campaign, do not forget to use the service together with other social media platforms. A good way to leverage your other external accounts is by promoting your Google Plus profile in these social media platforms. Consider Google Plus as a secondary platform or an accessory to Facebook or what not. Increase the visibility of your page by mentioning it in a post or a tweet.

4. Based on performance analytics, active users in various Google Plus communities respond well when faced with images especially photographs done by the pros. Take note of this when creating your content. But by no means should you resort to nothing else but copying images off of the Internet for your posts. Authenticity is very important here and users respond more to homegrown media.

5. One trick that many don't know is that you can make your posts more professional-looking not to mention more appealing by using operators such as * and _. And when tagging people, instead of the usual @, this particular platform uses +.

6. You can also use hashtags here. With Google Plus being a smallish community compared to its predecessors, you can find key influencers much easier on the platform. Get their attention, don't spam, and of course, be as respectful as possible.

Google Plus Best Practices

The beauty of this platform is that inexperience is not a drawback especially when you are building your online network. For as long as you keep your classy conduct, you will have no trouble generating a loyal following.

Again, when you create content for Google Plus, focus on how you can add value to the lives of those reading what you post. Give people something to be excited about and they will surely keep coming back for more.

See to it that you engage with your communities. Give them a reason to engage with your brand and always prepare a back-up conversation for your posts. Your objective is to get the word out regarding your business so get involved and be ready to answer any questions from your target audience. Because you expect them to respond and interact with you, meet them halfway and respond to their queries as soon as you can.

Scheduling Content on Google Plus

Timing is very important just like with other social media outlets. For this platform, most users log in at night so posting at around 6 to 9PM in the evening is a great place to start. As you continue testing your market, play around with different time settings until you find the best possible schedule for your feed. You can use third-party websites to schedule content here if you don't want to manually post content day after day.

Other Tools to Use with Google Plus

There are different tools that you should take advantage of especially if you are using Google Plus for the first time. As a business, you have a distinct demographic to target and a site by the name of Circle Count helps you by providing information on how the platform's demographics align with that of your brand.

This site checks millions of profiles and then they record the top influencers and measure your posts as to their responsiveness or composition using the former as a benchmark.

Part of using social media for business is measuring analytics to see whether or not a particular platform is effective. Google Plus had an in-platform service called Ripples that shows who shared and re-shared your content but it was removed in 2015.

These days, a third-party service called Simply Measured provides the same analytics data that can help you assess the relevance of your Google Plus page.

Chapter 8. LinkedIn

LinkedIn is a popular social network used more for professional connections rather than personal linkages. Just recently, it was purchased by powerhouse Microsoft for a whopping $26.2 billion. It is the world's largest professional social media platform that does not only link coworkers and colleagues but these individuals with businesses and potential employers as well.

Unlike ordinary job portals, this network allows community interaction and content sharing. Engagement is also faster compared to other job sites on the Internet. It has been highly effective for specific brands namely companies who are in the search for qualified manpower. After going through the details of what it offers and what you can do with LinkedIn, you can then decide for yourself if it is something that your business can benefit from.

Source: idagram.wordpress.com

The platform can be used in a variety of languages. Currently, it is programmed to run on 20 including Spanish, German, Portuguese, French, Italian, and of course, English. If you are running local operations, having a community profile set to your local language can be more effective as the platform can be used and understood by your targeted audience.

Platform Statistics

These days, there are about 300 million active users scattered across the globe. If your business is keen on reaching people on an international level then this will surely be an advantage. As much as 50 million endorsements are handed out via LinkedIn on a weekly basis. If you are looking for qualified personnel, this will help you narrow down your options with ease.

And with nearly 6 billion professional searches on record, you can see just how effective of a platform this is when it comes to manpower hunting. Aside from its growing list of users, you should know that there are millions of companies that have also listed themselves on this platform.

Did you know that LinkedIn delivers a conversion rate that is three times that of popular sites like Facebook and Twitter? This shows the potential, the opportunity, that you can take advantage of when it comes to this platform. But to benefit from its use, you should always keep your company page updated. Old content has no room here.

What People Do on LinkedIn

Users create personal profiles while companies create brand pages. In these profiles, personal users highlight their professional backgrounds and upload copies of their resumes. The platform, much like other social media sites, allow them to find connections up to the third degree and connect with these people. It can include everyone from the people that they know to those that they have actually worked with. Companies on the other hand create brand pages where they can post up-to-date employment opportunities for jobseekers to find.

All users are able to engage with one another and share content on the platform. If you take a closer look, you will see that content here are more industry-focused than personal. Through its community function, users have the ability to join groups that share a wide array of interests. It is a great platform for those in need of professional exposure and equally as advantageous to recruiters looking for the right people for their team.

Even if LinkedIn's primary purpose is to act as a recruitment platform, this does not mean that this is its only use. It is actually a great place where companies can boost their businesses through the use of different social activities. Business development here starts with the generation of B2B (business to business) leads.

Source: blog.linkedin.com

Creating and Using Your LinkedIn Account

Here are the steps that you need to follow to create your account:

1. Go to http://www.linkedin.com.

2. Enter your name, email address, and chosen password on the registration box.

3. Click the "Join Now" button.

4. Click on the "Confirm your email address" button to receive an email with a confirmation link.

5. Confirm your email and verify your account by clicking on the emailed link.

It is important that you create a powerful profile. Here's how:

1. Log into LinkedIn using your email address and chosen password.

2. Click on the Profile tab on the top left hand side of the interface.

3. Upload a cover photo.

4. Fill in the necessary details from your contact information to job experience.

Introduce your business by creating a page for it:

1. Look for the Interests tab at the top of the homepage.

2. Select the "Companies" tab.

3. Click "Create" in the "Create a Company Page" box that you will find on the right hand side.

4. Click "Continue" then proceed by entering the necessary details of your business.

5. Input a company description and a website URL as these are required before your page can be published.

LinkedIn Basics

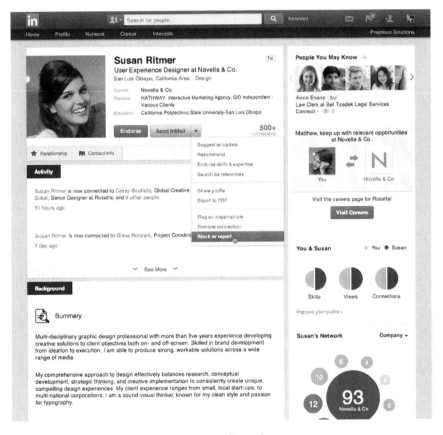

Source: www.techcrunch.com

1. Access your profile via the Profile tab.

2. Click on "My Network" to locate professional connections.

3. The "Jobs" tab will lead you to a list of available job posts from various companies.

4. The "Interests" tab will give you access to LinkedIn company pages, groups, and other learning tools.

5. You can access various business tools on the "Business Services" tab.

6. The message bubble will contain all your private messages.

7. The flag icon carries all of your recent notifications.

8. The person icon will show you potential contacts you might want to add or people who have requested to add you to their list of contacts.

9. Click on your profile image to access all administrative links on LinkedIn.

The Initial Approach

1. You can highlight your offerings here so highlight them. Focus your content on the products and services that you are offering and as much as possible, solicit recommendations for these. When people see what you have to offer and how these are of value to other users, they will find interest in them and may potentially try these out for themselves.

2. It is important that you establish your credibility not to mention build your brand up as an authority when it comes to your area of expertise. Develop a sense of trust among your customers and as you update your page and maintain your business presence, see to it that you

remain updated on relevant users' profiles and professional networks as well.

3. If you have a website with a working blog, you can add an RSS feed widget to your LinkedIn page. This will automatically show the feed to your followers especially when there has been a recent update to your blog. The platform also has a groups function so use this for engagement. Start meaningful conversations, offer advice, and answer queries. Keep in mind that groups are open to individual users, not brand pages.

LinkedIn Best Practices

1. Although self-promotion is important, do it sparingly. Overdo it and you will lose followers in the process. When you create your content plan, make sure that it discretely combines your brand promotion with valuable industry content.

   A simple "try this" message or "have you heard about our newest product" is enough. When you have managed to reel in interested parties, that's when you should elaborate more about the product you are advertising.

2. For effective business use, ensure that you complete your company page and update it as often as necessary. Any structural changes in the business or any sharable news tidbits should not be left in the dark. Visibility is very important.

   You might think that constant updates and content sharing may be daunting but keep in mind that every time you refresh your profile, your updates will appear in your followers' feeds.

3. Updating your profile and sharing content is just one piece of the puzzle. You also have to see to it that you

foster engagement and to do this, you should respond as soon as you can and as often as you can regardless of the comment left by a user.

Even if it's just to say thank you, a simple gesture like this will be well-received by the other end and will add to your brand's credibility online. If you answer queries, try to add value by offering advice or solutions to client issues.

4. Aside from gaining followers and accumulating business leads, you can also use LinkedIn to run an analysis on your competitors.Follow their pages and watch out for any updates they might have.

   This includes news about their companies, general product or service updates, and even any changes when it comes to their employee lineup. This will give you relevant information that you can use when developing your marketing strategies.

5. Because you are dealing with professionals, this means that you should be extra careful when it comes to whatever content you share, engagement lingo included. Unlike other social media networks, interactions here are not about immediate exchanges but a graceful buildup of relationships. This is how you avoid being tagged as a spammer.

   For sure you want to get your name out there but just like how it can be annoying when someone distributes tons of business cards at a professional gathering, sending out tons of invitations on LinkedIn can be detrimental instead of helpful to your brand.

6. If you genuinely want to get in touch with someone on the site, see to it that you send a personalized message. Introduce yourself and let them know why you are interested in connecting. Do not make the mistake of

telling them that it is because you are offering something for sale.

7. Also, if you are a community moderator, see to it that you monitor your community page for spam. Focus on having content that engages people, strikes relevant conversations, and builds interest in what you have to offer. This is how you can grow your community to levels which will be highly beneficial to your business.

8. When it comes to your community moderation and own content sharing efforts, it is always good to know what the latest and trending discussions are all about. If these relate to your brand and offerings then by all means use them.

    Under the Discussions tab on the dashboard, you can choose the "Latest Discussions" or "What's Happening" categories and this will show you the most recent activity and conversations on the site.

Chapter 9. Instagram

Social media marketing can be done in so many ways but there are certain platforms which are more effective than others. These days, one of the main platforms that you should not kick to the curb is Instagram as it is an important network especially for the younger demographic. It is a photo-sharing application that can be used across industries and has grown to become an invaluable tool for the establishment of a business' visual identity.

Although Instagram can be viewed on a desktop or laptop computer, it is mainly a mobile app. If you are new to Instagram for business, do not do anything without proper research. It would be good to test it out using a personal account first so that you can get a feel of how it works. Check out the profiles of the companies and brands which thrive on the platform. Check out the accounts of your competition too. Aside from competitive insights, you can gain a lot of inspiration by looking at successful accounts.

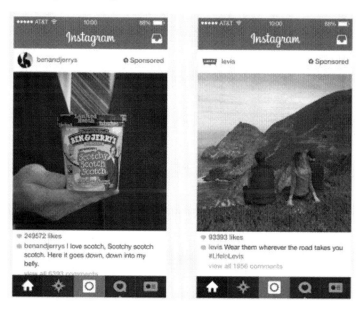

Source: techcrunch.com

Platform Statistics

There are plenty of opportunities that you can capitalize on when you make use of Instagram including a relatively high rate of engagement. It currently measures in at 4.21% per follower. This is equivalent to 58 times Facebook's average engagement and 120 times more than that of Twitter, two of the largest social networks in the world today.

Creating and Using Your Instagram Account

Here are some simple steps to get started:

1. Instagram is a mobile app so download it on your mobile device. You can find it on the Apple Store and Google Play. The best part about it is that the app is free.

2. All you have to do is sign up with a valid email. Once you are in, fill in your profile and do take enough time to finish this task. Be as professional and as truthful as possible and check everything twice.

3. Input a username then fill out the bio section. For your username, it would be best if it matched the name on your other social media pages. This will make it easier for people to find your account.

4. Add your profile photo, something larger than 110 pixels. This ensures that it appears in the right form either on mobile or desktop.

5. Do not forget to enable your notifications so that you will be alerted for likes, comments, and other relevant activity on your page. This will help you monitor the account efficiently ensuring that you don't miss out on anything important.

6. Finally, tell people you are out there by mentioning the account in your other live pages and also by following people on the platform.

Using Instagram is pretty simple and getting the hang of it will not take too much time. So have some fun, take notice of what is trending, and be as creative as you can with your images and captions.

To upload an image, here are the steps you need to follow:

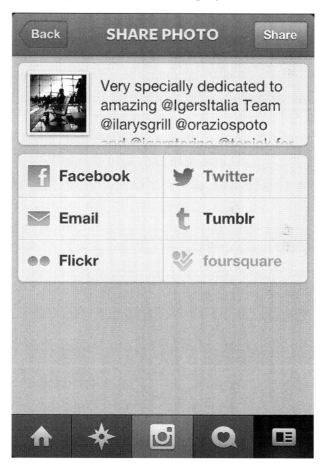

Source: blog.archie.co

1. Click on the camera icon to open your phone's image library.

2. Select the image and apply the necessary filters.

3. Add your caption.

4. Tag people.

5. Add a location.

6. Enable the sharing buttons (Facebook, Twitter, Tumblr, Flickr, and Swarm). Doing so, your Instagram post will also be published on your chosen social media platforms.

7. Click on "Share" to publish your image.

App Access Points

There are 10 important buttons that you will see on the app once you access it on your mobile device. Here are their functions:

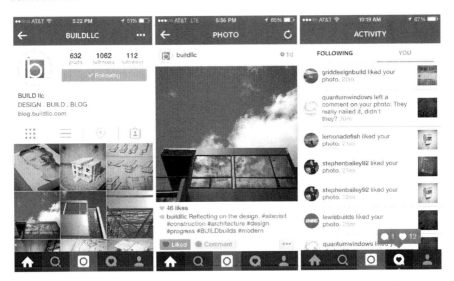

Source: blog.buildllc.com

1. Gear

   Provides access to all administrative options on the app.

2. 9-Dot Square

   Leads you to your image feed in grid form.

3. Lines

   Lead you to your image feed in list form.

4. Pin Locator

   Leads you to the mapped location of selected posts (if available).

5. Folder Icon

   Leads you to a page carrying your tagged photos from other uploaders.

6. Home Icon

   Leads you to your main Instagram feed.

7. Magnifying Glass Icon

   Leads you to the search function of the app.

8. Camera Icon

   Leads you to the image uploader.

9. Heart Icon

   Leads you to your notifications and activity log.

10. Person Icon

    Leads to your profile.

The Initial Approach

Once you have thoroughly familiarized yourself with the app, now is the time to create that marketing strategy. Think about the goals that you wish to achieve by using this social network. Make sure that these are in line with your general business goals. Do you want to increase traffic to your site or generate more sales? Are you interested in hashtag mentions or do you simply want more awareness for your brand?

All of the goals that you set for Instagram should be realistic, achievable, and of course, measurable. A simple tip: if you can't connect a goal with an action on Instagram, it will not be achievable. For example, if you can't tie your posts with the goal to increase eBook downloads, your efforts will end up zilch.

Identify your goals and then create your Instagram mission statement. This will be your guiding principle, what you will be basing your posts on. This will help you from using Instagram in the same way as Facebook or Twitter. These networks may seem to function in the same manner but they do carry distinct features that serve a specific purpose. In the case of Instagram, it has a powerful visual component where posts don't even have to contain heavy content to be relevant.

Implementing a Powerful Content Strategy

Your content strategy should revolve around posting frequency, times of day for posting, revolving content themes, and the establishment of a working content calendar. A regular posting schedule is important here since millions of images are posted per day. Content can easily get drowned in the process.

But there is a fine line between posting enough content within a day to bombarding users with posts. You don't want to fall within the latter category. Test your market and see which times of day they are most responsive. 2 to 3 images posted daily will be enough to start. One in the morning, midday, and in the evening.

One of the most important pillars of Instagram involves the proper choosing of subject matter and themes across accounts. As a business, you cannot simply post any type of content. You should focus on content that will help you establish and build your brand over time.

Focusing on Identifiable Brand Visuals

As what was previously mentioned, the platform is all about the visual element of things. This is why you should learn to create a cohesive brand identity through the use of appealing imagery – something that is not the easiest to do especially if you don't have a strong background in design.

Like other social channels, the themes, subjects, and designs you apply to your images should be reflective of the marketing strategy that you have already defined for the brand.

1. The first thing that you have to do is select a particular visual style. Instagram does not only function via separate posts. The way your profile feed looks, your personal archive of images, also matter.

    Since Instagram is popular for its filters, choose a couple that you will be using over and over again. If you do this, your feed will look as if your images were taken from a single rather than a series of sources. This ensures that your style will be recognizable online.

    If you are recognizable, you will have better chances of generating responses for your posts in the form of likes, shares, and comments. You can bet that the percentage of scroll-downs will consistently be lowered over time.

    People will not only be glancing at your images. They will actually spend time looking at it and sharing their insights giving you valuable information on their preferences.

2. Aside from the built-in image filters available on Instagram, it also offers basic image editing components from contrast to color settings. Private individuals actually use third-party apps to edit their images and so should you. Some of the best and simplest apps to use that will make your photographs look stunning include VSCO Cam and Whitagram.

Source: www.ha-ash.net

You can expect to gain access to more filters and editing elements from these apps. You can then save the edited images to your phone or directly import them to Instagram for posting.

3. Aside from the look of your Instagram account, you should also concern yourself with the focus that these images will follow. Having a clear theme reflected on the account will help your followers establish an online identity for your brand, something that they will easily recall.

Aside from ensuring that your theme is relevant to your brand, you should also see to it that your chosen theme will resonate with your target audience.

Instagram Best Practices

1. Although your content should focus on your brand, product, or service, be careful not to drown your followers in the same types of posts. Do mix in unique content every now and then. For example, your brand does not have to identify with being a lifestyle brand for you to post this type of content.

Aside from representing your brand directly, there is room for your Instagram to also be an online representation of your company's character and culture.

2. If you are new to this platform, you might not be all too familiar with how to identify your company image. Do not fret since you can gain inspiration by monitoring the accounts of your followers and fellow industry players.

Look at what is being shared and see if there are any trends that you can take advantage of. As you gain more information, you can start replicating the viable visual themes as you draft your content strategy.

3. You can post about the things your followers like and link it to your brand. For example, you can post about the perfect cup of coffee (provided that this is what your

followers like) and link it to the perfect accompaniment – the cookies you are selling perhaps.

4. Although the platform is highly visual, every post can be improved with the use of non-visual elements – captions. Again, this is something that will need your research for there are distinct languages and styles that should be applied to your posts depending on your target market.

   If they cannot understand or relate to what you are saying then the post is lost. You also need a main hashtag that will accompany your posts, one that is branded of course. But this does not mean that you should use your company's name. Think of it more as the need for a catchy tagline.

Chapter 10. YouTube

The creators of YouTube did not realize that they were in the process of launching a platform that will take over social media when they released it back in 2005. What started out as a haven for home video aficionados has transformed into one of the best social media marketing tools of the new generation.

Currently, it stands as the second largest search engine (Google being the first) and carries everything from home videos to tutorials to movie teasers, music videos, and so much more. It is a popular driver of modern online culture and has been an effective channel for Internet fame.

Platform Statistics

There are over a billion unique daily visits on the website with over 6 billion hours of video uploaded minute after minute. Most of its views are done via mobile with a recorded demographic of 18 to 34 year olds, both male and female, on an international scale. Many companies and private individuals are generating six-figure earnings from YouTube yearly making it an excellent marketing tool to test out.

Creating and Using Your YouTube Account

Source: www.lucrazon.com

Here are the steps to create your YouTube account:

1. Go to http://www.youtube.com and click the "Sign Up" link.

2. Input your email address and chosen password. Re-type these a second time to confirm.

3. Fill up the rest of the registration form with your personal information.

4. Type in the characters found in the word verification box for further identity checking.

5. Choose to select or deselect the box saying "Let others find my channel on YouTube if they have my email address." This gives you control over your uploads' privacy.

6. Check the "Terms of Use, Privacy Policy" box after going through the contents of the link.

7. Click "Create My Account" and you are all set.

To create a channel on your primary page, here are the things that you will have to do:

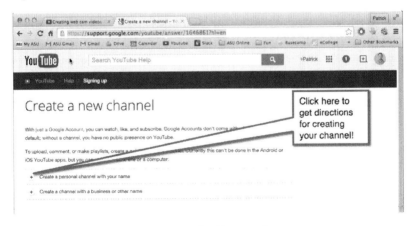

Source: teachonline.asu.edu

1. On your main dashboard, go to the "All My Channels" tab. You can choose to create a channel for a specific Google Plus page. You can also choose to create an independent channel.

2. Select the "create a channel" option then fill out the necessary details to create your channel. If you are creating a channel that will not be named after your Google Plus account, select the "choose a better name" option.

- Switching channels is easy and here's how to do it:

1. Switch between your main account and any desired channel by clicking the channel icon that can be found on the top right corner of the interface.

2. Choose the account that you want to use YouTube as from the available list.

Uploading videos

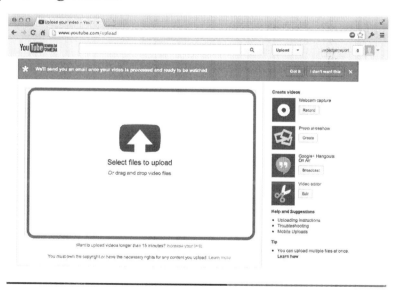

Source: tfortec.weebly.com

1. Sign into your account on YouTube.

2. Click on the upload button at the top of the interface.

3. Select the privacy settings for this upload.

4. Select a video to upload from your computer. You can also create an image slideshow if you wish or import photos from your Google Photos collection.

5. As the video uploads, edit the basic information and advanced settings.

6. Select "Publish" for a public video, "Done" for a private video, and "Share" to privately share your upload.

7. You can always publish your upload at a later time. For as long as you haven't clicked the "Publish" button, only you will be able to view the video.

8. For every upload, an email will be sent to you notifying you about it. You can choose to share this with your contacts for easy access.

The Initial Approach

Everyone that makes use of this social media network does so to share content. The way content moves through YouTube is pretty fast as videos are being shared at record rates. Users have the ability to follow a variety of channels and upload their own videos. They can leave comments and discuss footage and follow private individuals' content as well, for as long as the accounts have been set to public mode.

Source: www.keyword-suggestions.com

Aside from being a source of entertainment, it has become an excellent avenue for ad monetization. This makes the platform a financially sustainable resource for all users.

The kind of engagement that you will encounter in YouTube is something that you should be patient and careful about. The comments section below each upload can be a wasteland of sorts. You will find plenty of meaningless comments here. It is a good thing that as a brand, you have the option of turning off comments for your posts. It is suggested that you make use of this as often as you deem necessary.

When you start off with this platform, you can test the waters and leave the comments section on. This will give you an idea of what types of people view your uploads. This will also help you gauge engagement on this particular network.

You can manage the replies so if the comments that you get seem relevant to your brand then by all means keep them on. Just be patient when you encounter online trolls as there's no stopping them. If you see comments that are worth replying

71

to, respond. There are always more positive than negative effects when you choose to engage with your target audience.

Since YouTube has been purchased by Google, accounts can be linked together. Comments on YouTube uploads are also automatically linked with Google Plus accounts. If you are using the other platform, do link it with your YouTube page. To do this, you need to make your YouTube profile an administrator on your Google Plus page.

Simply log into the former and follow the instructions that will be provided to you by the site. Whenever there are alerts for new comments on your uploads, these will immediately appear on your notifications tab on Google Plus. You will also find a tab on your profile showing your YouTube videos.

Creating a Powerful Content Strategy

Over time, the platform has taken note of which uploads attract attention and which ones collect dust. Here is a basic approach to content that you should try out for the best initial outcome.

1. Regardless of which social media platform you choose for your marketing efforts, the importance of adding value via content cannot be stressed hard enough.

    With videos on YouTube, you can easily add value to a viewer's life by providing help content or how-to videos. You should apply what is known as a horizontal strategy.

    This means that aside from videos that are relatable to your brand, you should also have content that may not be directly connected to your offerings but may be of value to your targeted audience.

2. Do include exclusive content into your strategy as well. If you can provide your audience with early access to

your offerings or extend special promotions, by all means, do so.

3. If you are working with more than one product, you can create specific channels for each allowing your customers to have more than one channel to follow and more content to look forward to or share.

   This will help you engage with them more and add depth to the relationships that you are building over the Internet.

4. A good way to increase audience participation is by offering incentives. It can be in the form of product discounts or access passes to special events. You can use incentives to have your videos shared across media platforms.

   You can even create a special hashtag to go with these shares. This will engage the audience without you having to shell out a ton of money or increase your marketing workload.

5. Make sure that you create an appealing working title that is easy to search. For example, if you will be uploading a music video, the best format to use would be "Band Name - Song Title" as this is how most people would probably be searching for the song on search engines.

   Use keywords in your description to make it optimized but keep it short and sweet. This will make it easier for search bots and different users to locate your content.

As you apply these tactics to your social media plan, do not forget to measure your progress and your content's responsiveness. You should be mindful of what success looks like given the industry that you are in. Use this information to tailor your efforts towards strategies that will help you move forward and achieve your goals.

YouTube Best Practices

1. Engagement is a very valuable thing when it comes to social media and it is a vital component of YouTube marketing as well but do be sure to engage responsibly especially if you have enabled the comments setting on your uploads. Apart from monitoring them regularly, see to it that you stay engaged for as long as necessary.

2. Be mindful that this platform generates a ton of spam content so be patient. Always keep in mind that you are representing your brand, your company, so never lose your cool even in the presence of online trolls. When you make a comment, comment wisely, check your spelling, check your grammar, and of course, don't be a spammer too.

3. When it comes to advertising, although there are those who have generated significant revenues as a result of their efforts, not all who advertise on YouTube reap the same rewards. This is why you should carefully decide whether or not advertising is something necessary. If you have a high-volume channel then this could be promising but if not, it might be better to use your budget to advertise elsewhere and just focus on your content.

Other Tools on YouTube

Here are some of the tools that you can use to improve your efforts on YouTube.

1. Start by using YouTube TestTube. This helps you stay updated when it comes to the new features of the platform. It also gives you special access to limited-offer features when available.

2. And then there is YouTube Analytics that you can use to gain insights on your videos. From this you will know how they are performing and whether or not they are generating meaningful responses from your audience.

74

You will also gain relevant information on the demographics your content attracts.

3. If you want to know what you competitors are doing, you can use YouTube Advertisers which is a central hub which presents how other brands are utilizing the service. It is a great avenue for inspiration where you can learn a whole lot about effective content not to mention ad solutions. This is a great place to start if you are new to using YouTube for social media marketing.

4. Finally, you have YouTube Charts and it is basically a list of the popular and trending videos organized by criteria. If you want to be in the know then this resource is for you. From what is popular, you can generate similar content or re-share content that will appeal to your audience.

Chapter 11. Pinterest

Who would have thought that images on a digital corkboard would turn into one of the largest social media networks in the world? Aside from beautiful images from its users, the user-friendly pinning service is what attracted people to Pinterest.

It was launched in 2010 and has since been a go-to resource for image collectors. It covers everything from style to business to hobbies to special interests. It has also been a positive tool for businesses who are now able to connect with their users through vivid imagery.

Platform Statistics

With over 20 million active users per month, you can see just how much potential Pinterest has when it comes to social media marketing. With a network this huge, and growing by the minute, businesses can capitalize on a very wide customer reach.

In one month alone, the site gains an average of 50 million visitors. Daily pinned images average at about 5 million which is really massive. Imagine having several of these reflect your brand. Some social networks are favored equally by men and women, some more so by men, but with Pinterest, a majority of its audience is comprised of females.

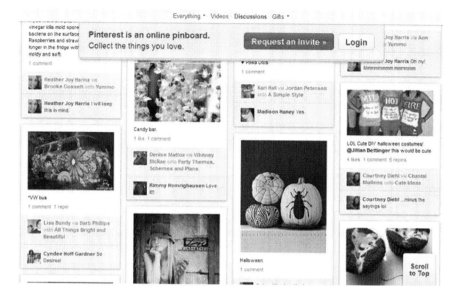

Source: www.responsemedia.com

The beauty of Pinterest is that it has the ability to influence purchases compared to other social media networks. Something featured on the site is more likely to be sold, and in bulk quantities, compared to something advertised on other platforms.

It is known to drive more referral traffic than any of its predecessors combined. If you are in the wholesale or retail business then this is something that is truly worth your while. The only thing you have to do is make an effort in taking amazing images that will capture the attention of pinners.

Creating and Using Your Pinterest Account

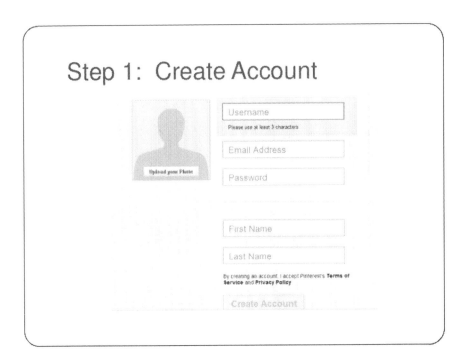

Here are the steps to create your Pinterest account:

1. Go to https://www.pinterest.com/business/create/.

2. Fill in your email, password, business name, website, and business type.

3. Click on "Come on in" to start the registration process.

4. Fill up the other required details then proceed with verification.

5. On the settings field, click on "Confirm Website."

6. Follow the instructions on the pop-up window. You have the option of verifying the site via an HTML file or meta tag. A verified site will mean that pins obtained from your account will bear your company's name and logo (added exposure on your part). You will also gain access to the web analytics page in Pinterest Analytics

giving you more detailed information on your page's activity.

7. Get the "Save" button to easily save images or pins from other sources for pinning or re-pinning on your own page.

Basic access points

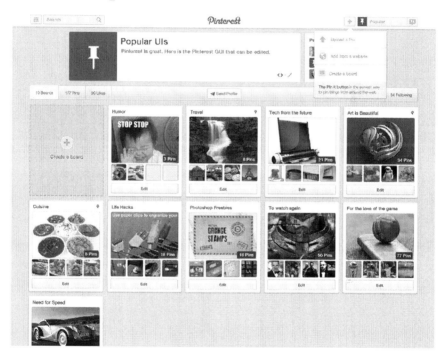

Source: lukechesser.github.io

1. Search for pins using the search bar on top of the interface.

2. Add pins by clicking on the plus icon on the right hand side.

3. Check your notifications by clicking on the icon beside the plus sign.

4. Click on your profile image to access your main page and manage your pins and boards.

5. Click on the Pinterest logo to refresh your feeds and see the most recent pins from your community.

6. Click on the analytics tab to check your page's activity and responsiveness.

The Initial Approach

With a growing community at your fingertips, you can easily engage with your target market via Pinterest. It is an excellent avenue for consumers to interact with brands so make it a point to regularly monitor your account and provide responses to any queries you may receive, good or bad.

It is also a good thing to leave a note of thanks every now and then and update your clients on any new development from your side. Start conversations and foster back-and-forth communication.

Also go the extra mile and check your page analytics to know how, when, and where your content is shared. This information will help you reach out to potential prospects that were not originally in your initial plan.

Creating a Powerful Content Strategy

For your initial content strategy, do consider these guidelines:

1. Start by highlighting your customer base. It is important that you know who is using your product or service. Read their stories to figure out how you can add value to their lives via your product. This might give you insights that you can use to make suggestions or advice.

2. People like to get noticed so acknowledge your audience and make them feel that they have, in turn, given you value. Engage with them and make them feel like they belong in your community. Inclusion will get you far in Pinterest.

3. As often as you can, give your audience a sneak peek into what happens inside the company or brand. Share something that will usually just remain behind closed doors.

4. You can provide interesting trivia or share images of your daily process. This does not mean that you should share your industry secrets. Just give them information, offered for a limited time, which will increase their feeling of getting something special for following you or spreading word about your brand.

5. If part of your operations includes charitable exposure or volunteerism, it will be a good idea to share this with your audience. Do not think of this as bragging. Aside from having people follow you because of their investment in your good deeds, you might also help out your charitable partners by recruiting new people for various causes.

6. As what was previously mentioned, know your audience. Aside from learning about which of your products they use and how often they use it, dig a little bit deeper into their lives and find out what they are interested in. This will help you create a social media plan that includes updates on things that will really resonate with them.

Source: redefiningdecor.com

7. The most important part of your strategy is to update your website and other social media accounts so that these can be shared with ease on Pinterest. Access and embed social sharing buttons to any business page you have direct access to. Improve your visibility and discoverability and your efforts will pay off tremendously.

8. When it comes to engagement, give credit where it is due. As you would like people to share your content, you are somehow expected to do the same so share others' content as often as you can. When pinning from the original source, see to it that you credit the original pinner.

9. If you will be linking a website to your Pinterest profile, do not forget to verify it. This will help you build your credibility online. By verifying your page, Pinterest will also have the ability to provide you with vital analytics showing you a record of pins pinned from your site, traffic information, and so much more.

Scheduling Content on Pinterest

When you share content, credit the source but change the captions to make it your own. Represent your brand well and ensure that your pin is relevant to the needs of your community. Remember that people are following you for a reason. Use appropriate keywords or hashtags, employ pin boards as well, so that people can easily locate your pins.

When pinning images, do so at different times of the day, not all at once, since this will be considered as flooding. When you pin at different hours, you are increasing your visibility across the platform as you are able to reach different audiences with ease. It also helps you avoid flooding your followers' pin streams, something that will encourage them to unfollow you over time.

When you employ pin boards, keep these as organized as possible. Any content that is irrelevant to the board has no place there. You should create a different board for every single piece of interest that falls under your brand's umbrella.

The platform also has a group board feature which you can use to collaborate with other people in providing unique content to the site's active users. If you want to target a small and specific audience, you can consider using a secret board. In this case, membership is by invite only. You may want to try it out for content sharing with coworkers.

Chapter 12. Tumblr

Have you ever tried Tumblr out, even on a personal level? Is your brand dependent on audiences that favor creative content? If your brand is best communicated via visuals then apart from Instagram, it would be best if you tested out Tumblr and took advantage of its largely untapped opportunity.

There is a large percentage of Tumblr users that uses the platform as a creative outlet. You will find plenty of users highlighting everything from writing to artwork so take advantage of this recurring theme. If you can provide an opportunity for your market to showcase their talents in relation to your brand, you will have a powerful campaign on your hands. Basically, offer the Tumblr community something that will be a challenge to ignore.

Platform Analytics

In fun and creative ways, you can reach new audiences with ease thanks to the 300 million unique monthly visitors that this platform consistently generated. Unlike other social media channels in which posts can easily get drowned out by massive content sharing, Tumblr has a feature that extends your post's life beyond a few days. This means that there is more time for people to see what you have to offer.

Source: www.businessinsider.com

Also, depending on your audience, this might be an excellent channel for you to test out. Let's say that your target demographic consists of people under the age of 35. Then this would simply be perfect. The site holds a lot of marketing potential and many businesses fail to see that hence their failure to capitalize on its ability to generate viral content in the blink of an eye.

With marketers extensively focusing their efforts on the Big 3 – Facebook, Twitter, and Instagram – they fail to reap the benefits of an important social media platform like this one. You can say that some might not be in the know as to what it can offer or some just don't know where to start when it comes to marketing to a Tumblr audience.

But to succeed on Tumblr, aside from familiarizing yourself with the platform and its features, it calls for pretty much the same things as other social media sites require starting with the provision of content that offers the right kind of value.

Source: www.digitalgov.gov

Creating and Using Your Tumblr Account

Here are the steps to creating your Tumblr account:

1. Go to http://www.tumblr.com.

2. Enter your email, password, and username.

3. Click "Sign Up" to start.

4. Generate your Tumblr page by uploading a profile image, adding a blog title, and inputting a description.

5. Click on "Make It" to generate your blog page. Choose blogs to follow afterwards.

There are several buttons on the dashboard and here are their functions:

1. Text – add text to your post

2. Photo – upload a photo to post

3. Quote – include a quote in your post

4. Link – embed a link into your post

5. Chat – chat with a fellow blogger

6. Audio – upload an audio file

7. Video – upload a video file

8. Eye icon – access the links that will enable you to customize your page

9. Heart icon – enables you to "like" a post

10. Double arrow icon – enables you to re-blog a post from another source

Tumblr Best Practices

1. If you will be using the site mainly for promotion, do not be a boring hard seller. What you want to do is generate content that will be appealing not to mention share-worthy.

   Do this by combining humor with your promotional posts. Generate good and healthy engagement through these posts and use them to drive traffic to your website. If you are not too pushy, you will win at this game so keep this tip in mind at all times.

2. If you will be utilizing sponsored posts, be sure to make these as innovative as possible. When you use paid posts, the content appears on the dashboards of active

users as promoted posts. Paid posts are there to do one thing that is to promote a product or service on Tumblr. Since it will be running on a limited time, you want it to generate the highest possible traction. To do this, don't resort to text or images alone.

3. Conceptualize video posts and use those. Based on research, video posts rake up the highest level of responsiveness across social media platforms. Especially with the kind of users Tumblr has, you want to provide something that is out of the ordinary if you want to get their attention.

4. So long as you keep your posts interesting, you will consistently be generating desirable levels of engagement on the site. Partner your posts with a memorable tagline. Keep posts short. Keep them clean. Every now and then, throw in a couple of memes to better fit into the community.

5. Finally, do spend the time to know your audience. Instead of treating the platform as just another social media website meant to help you promote your loins, use it as a means of providing value to the people that you want to follow you.

   There's nothing wrong about giving back. This will actually benefit you in the long run. Start by creating distinct content that appeals to the site's active users.

Give Tumblr users the kind of content that they can and will appreciate and you are good to go. The site's community wants attention thrown their way every now and then so don't hesitate to share the spotlight. Doing so will actually increase your engagements.

Given that Tumblr utilizes a different approach compared to other social sites, do give it time and spend time learning its features and functionality. The user dashboard is pretty simple to use so play around it before you launch the company page. It is a good idea to try it out for your personal usage first so that you can learn the ropes without having to compromise your brand image.

Chapter 13. Blogs

Does your business have a working blog? If you want to effectively market your brand via social media, you need to have a blog link on your website. For one, it helps drive traffic to your site. Plenty of people are online in search for information and an active blog is a great way for you to provide information. Surely you want more traffic to your site. Well, this is one of the best ways to gain that kind of traction.

Keep in mind that when people search for something online, they type something into their browser. People who know your business can simply enter your name but audiences you have yet to reach won't have you on their radar. It is fairly easy yet quite expensive to buy an email list. It will also require a ton of effort to reach these addresses one by one without the assurance that you efforts will lead to conversions.

You can also get more traffic by spending a whole lot of money on paid ads but once your budget is gone, so are your potential visitors. This is one of the reasons why organic traffic is still favored by many. Some might say that you simply have to update your page every now and then to stay relevant but how often can you really update your About Us page right? This is why you should consider blogging for your business as it solves these problems with ease. It provides you with an avenue to deliver fresh content as often as you deem necessary.

Each blog entry you generate means having another indexed page on your website which gives you more visibility on the Internet via search engines. Write interesting content with the right SEO keywords and your blog will be even more beneficial. The same content will also get you noticed via social media.

When people see what you've written and find interest in it, they can easily share it with their social media networks where their connections can re-share the same links over and over again. Exponential exposure is what you can expect from this.

Having a blog can also help you drive traffic and improve conversion. The more people know who you are, the greater potential there is for new clients to surface. The trick to increasing conversions via blog is by adding a clear yet concise call to action to your entries. Do this for all of your posts. You can offer free resources like webinars, fact sheets, or even free trials in exchange for contact information like email or a phone number. Offer an incentive and you will experience a boost in leads. In addition, people would be more likely to try what you offer.

But make sure that you don't expect all visitors to buy something. This is simply unrealistic. The most important thing is that people become aware of who you are and what your brand has to offer. Who knows? Someday, they might find your offering essential. At least they will have the necessary brand recall.

Have a working blog and enable yourself to establish your authority online. The more you add value to a prospect's life, the more your content helps people out, the better it will be for your brand. It will stick in people's minds that you are the go-to brand for essential information and the like. A good gauge of what you should be writing about is the common concerns and questions of your target market in relation to your products or services.

Blogging also drives long-term results as the people that see your content accumulates over time after you release each blog entry. It will appear consistently in search engines months, even years, after it was first published. This means that there is always a way for each entry to help you generate visitors, leads, and conversions. Basically, it is not a one-time thing.

Blogging also has its smaller, but still relevant, benefits like the provision of a test page for a campaign that you might be planning to launch on the Internet. Before you invest time, money, and effort into the actual strategy, you can get a feel of how people will respond to it by releasing a blog entry. Blogs can also be used by companies as a PR tool where news, updates, and important information about products and services can be released.

If you have started a blog yet don't know where to start when it comes to your content, here are a few things that may help you out. Before you go all out with the writing, you should start with a comprehensive plan, a content marketing strategy if you will. It is quite simple to do so. Keep in mind though that blogging does not deliver instant results. It will surely take some time before you reach a desirable level of momentum.

Never consciously choose to wing it when blogging as you will be setting yourself up to fail. With every blog entry you make, see to it that you write it in the best possible way with all of the pertinent information and SEO keywords inputted into the page. Start with some ample research so that you can build a solid foundation not only on your market but the industry that you are swimming in as well. This will help you blog more often and do so effectively.

Read other blogs for inspiration. You can read a combination of blogs from personal accounts to business or brand-related ones. This will give you insights into how best to write given different sets of audiences. After viewing these blog sites, find a couple that your brand can relate with and use these as your models. This will help you figure out the right representation for your business. Consider blogs that have been around for at least half a year and have been consistently publishing content.

Do not hesitate to check the blogs of your competitors. They might have a strategy in play that you can also use for your own company. In this case, they've already done most of the work. You can cut back on the time you spend on trial and error studies and simply reap the rewards of their efforts.

Part of creating a blog is creating a mission statement for your brand. The first question that you need to answer is why you are creating a blog for your business. If you have figured this out then focus on what you should be writing about. There should be a clear purpose as to why you are engaging in such a strategy.

To identify what you should be writing about, answer three more questions starting with who your target market is. Who are the people that you deem as prospective clients? What demographics of people do you wish to attract? Second is what types of information do these people need. By answering this, you are somewhat identifying what types of content you should be focusing on. How can you add value to their lives through your products or services? Present this in a creative and interesting manner through your blog entries.

Finally, ask yourself how you can help these people out. Yes, a blog, even if it one for business, should not be purely focused on the brand and selling its offerings. You should create content that people will come back to you for. Tutorial videos, how-to's, and funny bits, are excellent in attracting positive attention.

Your readers are smart and they can tell if a company is merely concerned with trying to sell them something or actually interested in giving them value for free. Not everything in business revolves around money especially when it comes to social media marketing.

Your main marketing strategy should be consistent across all platforms, blogging included. Don't have a separate list of marketing goals for your blog to achieve. It should be complementary effort to your primary marketing tactics. For example, whenever you create a new blog entry, use it to populate your social media accounts. This is how you can effectively grow your business. Do the opposite and you will simply be wasting your time. You can also send these blogs to your prospects as a follow-up when you've had your meetings.

A blog also has to have a schedule. You don't have to burden yourself by releasing blog entries day after day. Test out how responsive your content is and slowly determine how often you should be publishing content and on which days of the week. Set a meaningful schedule and as you gain more readers, that's when you can increase your posts.

Chapter 14. Social Bookmarking Websites

There are websites that are classified as social bookmarking sites. This means that their main purpose is to help people with social media promotion. Some of the best social bookmarkers are Reddit, Digg, and StumbleUpon. These sites work by collecting shareable self-uploaded content from their users. They then curate these and organize the links leading to the different uploader websites.

This kind of process is crowdsourced. Aside from self-uploading content, users are also able to prioritize links, sort them, and classify them into various categories. These pages have a relatively large following with links shared across the community. Smaller websites can generate flash crowds with ease. This just shows you how strong and powerful these bookmarking sites are.

These pages also offer advertising which can be placed in specific communities or category pages. Ads are not offered by the websites themselves but have been coded to accept placements from third-party providers like Google pay per click (PPCs).

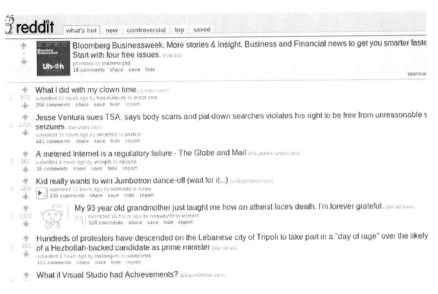

Source: alexrecker.com

Chapter 15. Beyond Published Content: Advertising on Social Media

You can further increase the traction or results of your social media marketing efforts by allotting a certain portion of your working budget to social media ads. If you scan various social media feeds, you will see that there are sponsored posts that come up every now and then. Depending on the platform, you will have different ad options to choose from.

These days, active advertising can be done on Facebook, Instagram, YouTube, Yelp, and Tumblr. Ads are displayed across relevant feeds, based on the demographics you input into the ad manager. You can choose to exclude current followers so that your budget goes into finding new potential followers for your account.

Ads on Facebook are created based on the objective that you wish to achieve:

1. Awareness

☐   Reach people near your business

If your business relies more on walk-in clients then this is a great place to start. Businesses like boutique stores, restaurants, and cafes will find this ad quite useful.

☐   Boost your posts

Check the insights portion of your profile and you will see which of your posts gained the most responses or engagement from your followers. It is a good idea to boost this post, have it displayed on feeds as an ad, as it may attract new followers or "likers" to your page.

☐   Promote your page

This is the basic "Like my Page" ad where you can give a short description as to why people should follow your page. A good tip would be to state what you have to offer. Be direct and keep your message concise.

2. Consideration:

☐   Raise attendance at your event

Have an upcoming event? Why not use the platform with billions of users to advertise it? With a large number of people using Facebook daily, this will ensure that you reach as many relevant individuals as possible. Not only is it cheaper than traditional TV, radio, or print ads but it is more effective than all three combined.

☐   Collect leads for your business

If you need leads for your business, you can ask people, through ads, to sign up for your website or any online page that you may have. This will help you generate a client list with ease.

☐   Get video views

Have a new company or product video that you would like your target market to see? Release it via an ad through your Facebook account.

☐   Get installs of your app

If you have a newly developed app that you want people to download and test out, you can actively advertise it on Facebook.

☐   Send people to your website

This works like the "Likes" ad but instead of increasing the visibility of your Facebook page, you can increase the visibility of your website or a specific page on your website.

3. Conversion:

☐   Get people to claim your offer

Do you plan on promoting your brand or product through a giveaway offer? Then this is the kind of ad that you should use.

☐   Increase conversions on your website

Want to turn site visits into actual sales? This is the kind of ad that you should be focusing on.

☐   Increase engagement in your app

Get feedback and insights on your app. Know what users are thinking about the service with this particular ad.

After choosing the objective, you then have to customize your audience by country, demographic, and interests. This is followed by you choosing a placement for your ads. Ads on Facebook can be set to run on Instagram, mobile news feed, desktop news feed, and right column display.

When you are fine with the audience and placement, it is now time to set a desired daily budget and schedule. There is a $1 minimum for an ad's daily budget but there is no limit as to how long you can run it. The next move is for you to work on the creative element of your ad.

You can add one to a series of images or choose to upload a video for your ad. There are text provision boxes as well where you can input attention-grabbing headlines and ad body messages. Finish your ad off with a specified call to action and place your order.

For YouTube, you can apply two types of video ads, one that runs for a full 30 seconds or more, or one that allows viewers to skip it after a 5-second showing. Ads on YouTube cost depending on the engagement. If the full ad is shown there is a charge for impressions but if it is skipped before it runs its course, it is free.

Yelp offers more basic advertising in the form of a featured listing on the search page. Basically, establishments that decide to run ads will have their business positioned as the first result on the generated search list. They also have the advantage of having the ads of their competitors removed from display from any of their own listings. Ads are paid on a per-click basis so you get the advantage of free impressions on the Internet.

Finally, there is Tumblr. There are four types of ads available to Tumblr users. First, there is the sponsored mobile post wherein the advertiser's blog posts will appear on users' dashboards when they are online via a mobile device like a Smartphone or tablet.

Here, the users can like, share, or even re-blog the post. You can also take advantage of a sponsored web post which works in the same way with the difference being that the advertiser's posts will be viewable on a desktop or laptop computer.

Third-party ad extensions are also available from Tumblr. You can use sponsored Radar ads. Radar works by scanning the entire Tumblr community picking the most creative not to mention original posts it finds. These posts are then placed on the right side of the screen next to the main dashboard. Based on analytics, these posts generate as much as 120 million daily impressions.

If this wasn't enough, you can also utilize sponsored Spotlight posts. Spotlight acts as a directory service for the most popular blogs on the platform. It makes use of fifty categories to classify the blogs and advertisers can choose one of these for their blog to be listed on. The lists generated by Spotlight provide advertisers with an excellent avenue for their site to be visible as many users check these out for new blogs to follow.

There are plenty of opportunities to reach a wide audience through social media with the help of ads. It would be best to use these in conjunction with engaging content generating a good balance between paid and organic content. Especially if you are new to social media marketing, this is a cost-effective way to advertise on the Internet.

Facebook ads are the simplest ones to program and test so this is a good place to start if you are new to the social media marketing scene. A good test run for an ad would be 3 days but make sure that you are deploying ads on weekdays as weekend traction tends to run quite slow.

It is also a good idea to run test ads for one product side by side so that you can see which one works better for your targeted market. Over time, even the best ads can suffer from ad fatigue. If this happens, start your tweaks by editing the creatives for your ad sets. As you gain more experience with the platform, you might want to create custom audiences for a narrower target. Regardless of the platform that you use, check your ads on a weekly basis and make as many adjustments as necessary.

Chapter 16. Social Media Marketing Metrics

There are different methods to measure your engagement on social media. You can get metrics from website reports which track leads and the volume of visits your pages receive. There are free tools like Google Analytics that you can use to get this information and study consumer behavior from response demographics to what types of devices they use.

Of course the primary reason that you will have to venture into social media marketing is to generate sales. Social media is a very useful advertising tool but there is always the challenge of quantifying how much it contributes to your profits.

When it comes to the return on your investment, you can measure it using market analytics or by comparing your marketing efforts to the sales activities you are getting but these won't render 100% full-on data. What you will get is an idea of how well your social media presence is contributing to the success of your brand.

Social media exposure can also give you relevant market data when it comes to consumer sentiment. A number of consumers resort to social media to air their concerns, both positive and negative, over brands and their offerings.

With this information, companies have the ability to know first-hand how their products or services are being viewed by their prospects. Using this data, they now have the chance to improve on their offering or adjust their marketing strategy. The best thing about this is that vital information can be obtained within seconds.

Conclusion

Social media marketing has surely revolutionized the way people do business these days and more companies are joining the bandwagon and getting their brand out there. It is a great tool to use especially for starter businesses as it is cost-effective and proven to be highly effective.

What is important is that you study how the different platforms work and understand how their varying features can be used to your advantage. As these technologies are constantly being updated, it is a good thing to always be in the know. Research on the different platforms and be mindful of updates. Everything can be found online so do not hesitate to run a couple of searches here and there. The more you know and understand about a platform and its functionality, the better you can design your campaigns to be.

There are plenty of social media platforms that you can utilize but this does not mean that you should focus your attention on all of them. You need not utilize every single one to succeed in your social media marketing attempt. Test them out to see which one works best and focus on the ones which are most promising.

If you are just starting, be patient as it will take some time to perfect your online marketing strategy. Do not be afraid to test out various forms of media from text to images to videos. Listen to your market as they have the final word. It is not about what you want but what they want. Remember that their support is what you need to get the sales that you desire.

Different platforms have different tools, free and paid, that you will gain access to. This will give you more flexibility as you draw up those marketing campaigns. Start your efforts with the free services then use the paid features when you find the need for them. It would be best for you not to immediately jump into using the paid features if you can generate the same traction without having to pay a single cent.

With social media marketing, there are tricks and styles that you will learn over time that will help you build and maintain a reputable and credible online presence. It will involve continuous learning especially since the technology has the tendency of changing day after day. You should keep up with these updates and never lose track of your progress. This is how you will succeed in this avenue of marketing.

Most importantly, don't be afraid to test the waters. There are tons of benefits that you will be able to enjoy when you take your business online and on social media. It provides you with the greatest exposure compared to other styles of and marketing channels. Not only that but it offers the most cost-effective not to mention convenient way of reaching your market in these ever-changing times.

I hope you have learned plenty from this book. The next thing to do would be to kick start your social media marketing efforts for your business.

Finally, if you enjoyed this book, please take the time to share your thoughts and post a positive review on Amazon. It'd be greatly appreciated!

Thank you and good luck!

26477402R00065

Printed in Great Britain
by Amazon